songs for a new world

MUSIC & LYRICS BY JASON ROBERT BROWN

Will Young

Songs for a New World was recorded for release on BMG Classics

ISBN 0-634-03578-9

HAL•LEONARD®
CORPORATION
7777 W. BLUEMOUND RD. P.O. BOX 13819 MILWAUKEE, WI 53213

Visit Hal Leonard Online at
www.halleonard.com

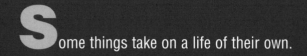

Some things take on a life of their own.

I was 20 years old when I got to New York City, and I was determined to write my big Broadway musical. The only problem was that I didn't really know anybody in New York other than the delivery guy from the Chinese restaurant, and I didn't think he would be such a great collaborator, since he couldn't even give me the right change. So I decided I would just take a bunch of songs I had written for various abandoned pieces and put them up at a cabaret, and I could find collaborators from there. But some things take on a life of their own, and I couldn't stop working on this material.

Then I met Daisy Prince at a piano bar where I was working, and she came to see the show, and she seemed to really like it, and so out of nowhere, I asked her if she wanted to direct it. I had never seen Daisy direct so much as traffic—there are just times when my intuitions are really strong, and if I'm lucky, I pay attention: in this case, I was lucky, and Daisy said it sounded like fun. She asked me to write an opening number to say what the show was going to be about.

So we started working, and working, and working, and eventually, Daisy and I had been working on *Songs for a New World* for three years, and we still didn't have an opening number.

Now, as far as we were concerned, *Songs for a New World* was still just going to be a collection of my cabaret and theatre songs, a way to introduce my writing to the world. But the show had become more than that—it was starting to take a strange new shape, and Daisy and I were powerless to control it: somehow, songs that had always been perfect on their own seemed awkward in context; songs that had been written years and miles apart seemed to make sense together; words and melodies that came from different times and places all seemed to add up to one statement. We had discarded piles of songs—I don't know why they weren't right, but I know they weren't—and new songs had been written to replace them. And there we were, doing a workshop in Toronto, and we needed an opening number to say what this show had turned into, what *Songs for a New World* was really about.

It's about one moment. It's about hitting the wall and having to make a choice, or take a stand, or turn around and go back. I hadn't realized that that was what it was about, but I sat down at the piano in the rehearsal room at 1:30 in the morning, and suddenly I knew. The moment you think you know where you stand, the things that you're sure of slip from your hand, and you're suddenly a stranger in some completely different land.

A year later, we opened at the WPA Theatre, with four brilliant performers, a five-piece band, and an unbelievably talented group of designers finally bringing my songs to life.

The set for *Songs for a New World* looked like a combination of the deck of a ship and a playground—a vast wooden space with platforms and stairs and ropes, and hidden treasures. It played only 28 performances at the WPA, a standard run there, but represented for me one of the only times in my life so far where something actually felt like it was supposed to. I guess when a show isn't a big commercial success, the general temptation is to keep working on it, to fix it, to make it "right"— I've never had that urge with this show; it may not have been everybody's bag, but I know we nailed it: every actor, every musician, every one of Brian Besterman's orchestrations, every inch of Gail Brassard's costumes and Stephan Olson's scenery, every cue of Craig Evans' lighting and Jim Bay and John Curvan's sound design, every step of Michael Arnold's choreography, every laugh and ovation—they were all just as good or better than they were when I dreamed about them. All under the extraordinarily talented direction of Daisy Prince, a phenomenal collaborator in every way.

It occurs to me that *Songs for a New World* is a pretty good summation of the first 25 years of my life, and especially my first five years in New York City—maybe that's what it's really about after all. I realize that not every composer gets to have his first show in New York be such a magical experience, and I know how lucky I am. What I also know is how little of the entire experience I actually had any control over; some things take on a life of their own, and if you're smart, you trust in the moment, hold your breath, and sail away.

Jason Robert Brown
© 1996

CONTENTS

The New World

Music and Lyrics by
JASON ROBERT BROWN

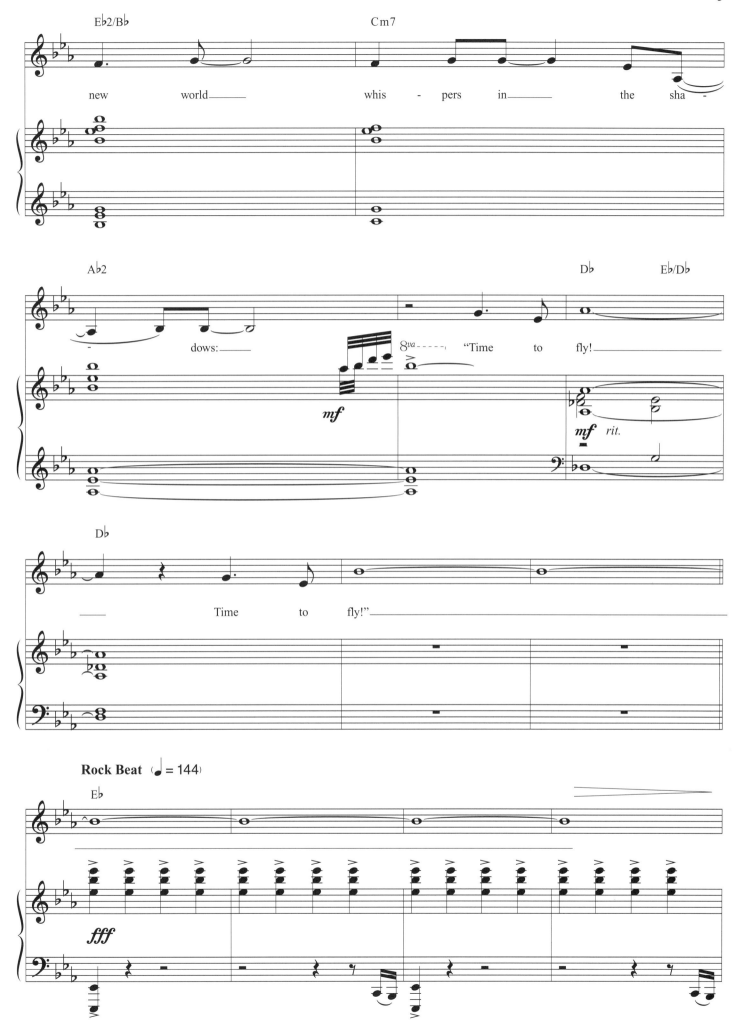

MAN 2:

It's a-bout one mo - ment, The

mo - ment be - fore it all_____ be - comes clear; And in that

one mo - ment, You start to be - lieve there's no -

14

20

I'm Not Afraid of Anything

Music and Lyrics by
JASON ROBERT BROWN

Moderate Folk Rock

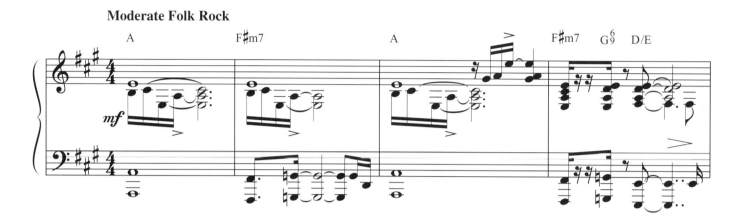

Jen-nie's a-fraid — of wa-ter, — I mean, she swims — so well, — but still, she's a-fraid of wa-

— ter. — So she won't go near — the sea... —

24

Stars and the Moon

Music and Lyrics by
JASON ROBERT BROWN

I met a man with-out a dol-lar to his name,— who— had no

traits of an-y val - ue but his smile

She Cries

Music and Lyrics by
JASON ROBERT BROWN

Moderately Fast

There's a cou-ple of things___ I've learned___ on the man-y roads___ I've ta-ken:

Flames are not what get____ you burned;____ it's the cold____ and the ice.____

Here's a piece____ of ad - vice____ that I got____ from a lit - tle bird:____ The

flames____ can____ get you stirred; it's the cold____ that leaves you

shak - en.

mp

48

no one can make_____ you for - get how you feel;_____ for

all she can take,_____ you've got more there to steal. So you don't mind a bit_____ of sur-

prise..._____ and she cries._____

I don't like to ad-mit I'm wrong.___ I be-lieve in guts___ and glo - ry.

mp

But it's time___ I should change___ my song;___ I've been here___ just a bit___ too long.___

Surabaya-Santa

Music and Lyrics by
JASON ROBERT BROWN
Additional Material by
KRISTINE ZBORNIK

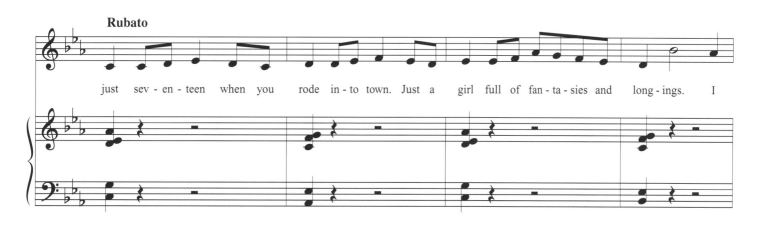

Rubato

looked in my eyes and you asked me my name, and I trem - bled be - fore you like a ba - by and

gen - tly I kissed you. *8va* (Who could re - sist you?)

a tempo

You took me heart and soul. And be -

gliss.

fore I had a chance to take con - trol, we re - tir - ed to your pal - ace on the

sit by your-self on the couch in the den, and you watch *Mir-a-cle on Thir-ty Fourth Street...* You

get sad and dream - y, can't e - ven see me,

won't e - ven say "hel - lo." _____ Now you

rall. *gliss.* *a tempo*

tell me that it's time for you to go. Sling your sack up - on your back and "ho - ho -

I don't sup - pose you'd ev - er want me⎯ by your side.

I know you now; you want a play - thing, not a bride. So on your

way, Nick. Sha - lom, Nick. Don't feel the need to hur - ry home, Nick!

Should I need com - fort in a cold and⎯ bit - ter storm,

I've got the elves to keep me warm.

Spoken: *Oh Nick! Nick, I didn't mean it! I'm just going crazy…*

…all cooped up in here.   *Oh, Nick!*

Please take me with you.   *Please, I'm your wife, damn it.*   *Isn't there one ounce of human…*

When you re-turn I will be man-y miles a - way.

I'll have my law-yer call your law-yer New Year's Day. That's all for

me, Nick. Gang - way, Nick. I'll miss you less than I can say, Nick!

Have fun with all the lit - tle boys a - long your route.

74

Christmas Lullaby

Music and Lyrics by
JASON ROBERT BROWN

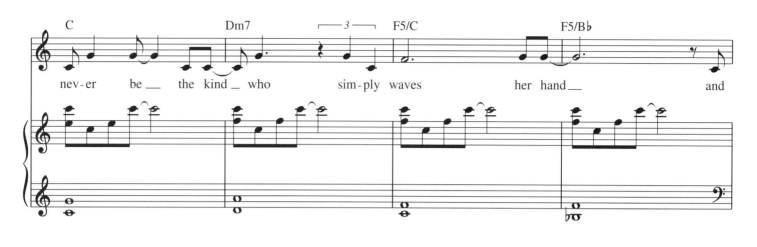

nev-er be __ the kind __ who sim-ply waves her hand__ and

has a mil-lion peo-ple do____ the things I wish_ I'd done._ But in the eyes_

Warmly, poco rubato

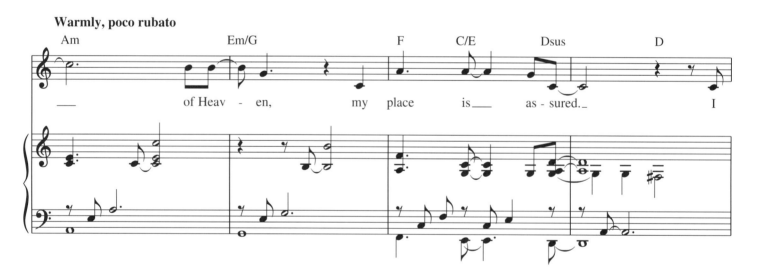

__ of Heav-en, my place is__ as-sured._ I

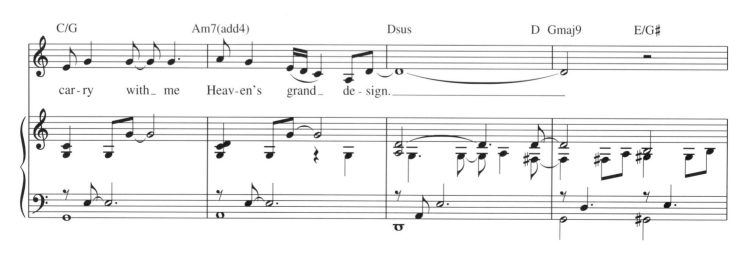

car-ry with_ me Heav-en's grand_ de-sign._____

Dm7(add4) C(add9)/E B♭ Am7 Gsus C5/F
mp
-ry with a bless-ing in my soul, and the fu-ture of the world in-side of me.
mp
C Dm7 F5/C F5/B♭ C(add9)
bring out; lyrically
Dm7 F(add9) G7sus E/G♯ Am(add2) Em/G
mf
In the eyes of Heav-en, my
rich and warm
mf
F C/E Dsus D C(add2)/G Am7sus Am
place is as-sured. I car-ry with me Heav-en's grand de-sign.

King of the World

Music and Lyrics by
JASON ROBERT BROWN

I'd Give It All For You

Music and Lyrics by
JASON ROBERT BROWN

MAN:
I had a house while you were gone.—

The week af - ter you left me, I found a cou - ple a - cres

95

102

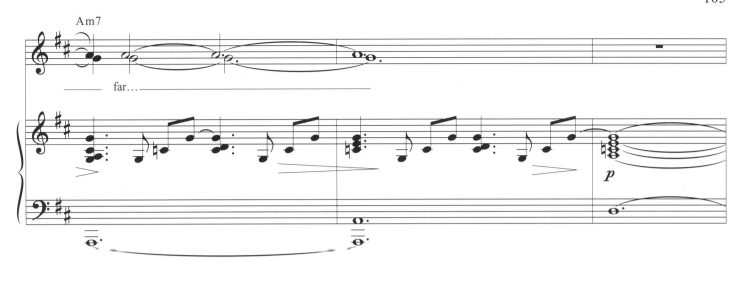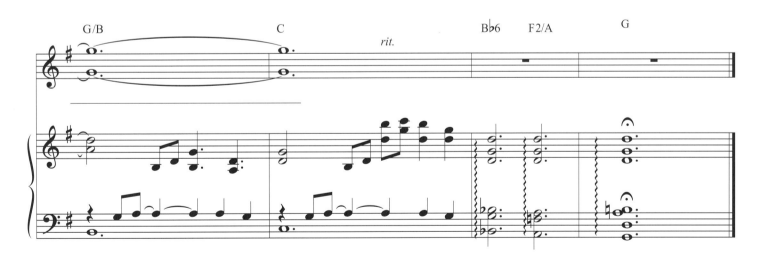

The Flagmaker, 1775

Music and Lyrics by
JASON ROBERT BROWN

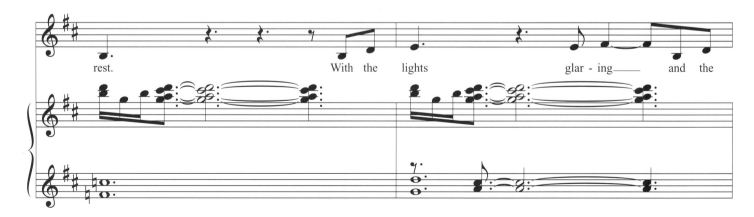

ten - sion in - side o - ver - flows and goes too far,_____ one more

star, one more stripe, to es - cape your lone - ly bed. One more

star, one more stripe. Join the blue, the white, and red. One more

star, one more_____ stripe, as you pray your child's not

last let - ter_____ says he's fight - ing in a

ditch. Then the can - dle flick-ers_____ and the

riv - er bick-ers,_____ What else can you do but

stitch_____ one more

112

Hear My Song
(Solo version)

Music and Lyrics by
JASON ROBERT BROWN

122